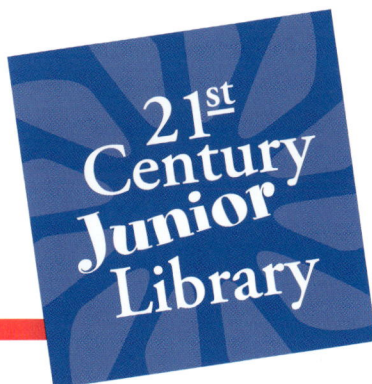

21st Century Junior Library

Saws

by Katie Marsico

CHERRY LAKE PUBLISHING * ANN ARBOR, MICHIGAN

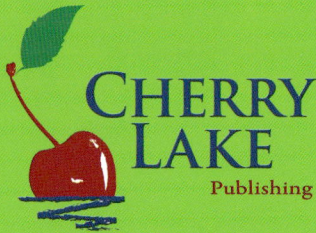

CHERRY LAKE
Publishing

Published in the United States of America by Cherry Lake Publishing
Ann Arbor, Michigan
www.cherrylakepublishing.com

Content Adviser: Roger McGregor, Director, Hannibal Career & Technical Center, Hannibal, Missouri

Reading Adviser: Marla Conn, ReadAbility, Inc.

Photo Credits: Cover, ©Pressmaster/Shutterstock, Inc.; page 4, ©Denis and Yulia Pogostins/Shutterstock, Inc.; page 6, ©Maryna Pleshkun/Shutterstock, Inc.; page 8, ©iStockphoto.com/AdShooter; page 10, ©auremar/Shuttersstock, Inc.; page 12, ©Konstantin Gushcha/Shutterstock, Inc.; page 14, ©Dikiiy/Shutterstock.com; page 16, ©Stocksnapper/Shutterstock, Inc.; page 18, ©Christina Richards/Shutterstock, Inc.; page 20, ©photomak/Shutterstock, Inc.

LIBRARY OF CONGRESS CATALOGING-IN-PUBLICATION DATA

Marsico, Katie, 1980–
   Saws/by Katie Marsico.
      pages cm.—(Basic tools) (21st century junior library)
   Audience: K to grade 3.
   Includes bibliographical references and index.
   ISBN 978-1-62431-171-0 (library binding)—ISBN 978-1-62431-303-5 (paperback)—
ISBN 978-1-62431-237-3 (e-book)
   1. Saws—Juvenile literature. I. Title.
   TJ1233.M37 2013
   621.9'34—dc23   2013007049

*Cherry Lake Publishing would like to acknowledge the work of
The Partnership for 21st Century Skills.
Please visit www.p21.org for more information.*

Printed in the United States of America
Corporate Graphics Inc.
July 2013
CLFA13

CONTENTS

A saw is a useful tool if a tree in your backyard needs trimming.

4

What Is a Saw?

Have you ever seen someone cut a piece of wood? Have you watched a person trim a tree branch? Maybe you have been to a machine shop. Did you see a worker there slice through a strip of metal? If so, you have probably watched someone using a saw.

Sometimes handsaws have plastic handles.

A saw is a cutting tool. You are probably most familiar with a handsaw. Handsaws usually have a wooden handle. They also have a **serrated** steel blade. A serrated blade has a jagged edge. Its steel blade is carved into a row of notches, or teeth. These teeth point outward.

Make a Guess!

How do people use saws at home? Why would they use saws to cut through certain materials? What materials would they cut with scissors or knives instead?

Jigsaws are a kind of power saw that can be used to cut shapes in wood.

Handsaws are powered only by a person's arms and hands. Other saws run on machine power. These saws are called power saws. A power saw has a **motor**. The motor often relies on electrical, steam, or water power.

Some saws have sharp teeth that cut through pipe.

How Are Saws Used?

Someone using a handsaw holds onto the handle. He or she places the blade against material that will be cut. The person then moves the saw back and forth. The blade's teeth pass over the material's surface. This creates a cut as the material wears away.

Saws with spinning blades such as this one are called circular saws.

A person usually uses a forward and backward motion with a handsaw. Not all saws operate the same way though. For example, some feature serrated blades that spin. Others have blades that move straight up and down.

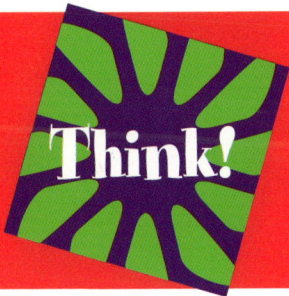

Think!

Study the blades on two or three different saws. Think about which ones would be best for cutting certain materials. Picking the right tool makes a worker's job much easier!

Computers can help make woodworking, such as making furniture, more exact.

Not every saw involves someone holding a handle. Sometimes a person uses a computer to control a saw's movement. These kinds of saws are usually used in machine shops and factories.

A miter box can be used with a backsaw to create slots in a piece of wood. Then the saw does not cut all the way through the wood.

Different Kinds of Saws

Saws come in many shapes and sizes. Certain handsaws are very small. Backsaws might be as long as a toothbrush. They are good for slicing through thin plastic. The world's largest saw stretches as tall as a lighthouse. It is used to cut **coal** out of the ground.

Concrete saws are tough enough to cut into paved roads and sidewalks.

Many people work with crosscut saws and ripsaws. These handsaws are good for home projects involving wood. Other saws cut through tougher material. **Concrete** saws have spinning circular blades. The blades are often made from diamonds. These hard stones can slice through concrete and brick.

It is important to use safety gear when working with a power saw.

Do you need something cut with a saw? Do not do it yourself. Always have an adult operate a saw. Some people have had serious accidents. Often, they did not know how to use a saw correctly. Saws can be dangerous. Yet they help us cut everything from tree branches to bricks. That would be much harder without these important tools!

Look!

Do your parents own any saws? Ask to see them. Find out what kind of things they cut with each different saw!

GLOSSARY

coal (KOHL) a black mineral formed from the remains of ancient plants; coal is mined underground and burned as a fuel

concrete (KON-kreet) a building material made from a mixture of sand, gravel, cement, and water, which becomes very hard when it dries

motor (MOH-tur) a machine that supplies power to make something run or move

serrated (SER-ay-tid) having a jagged edge

FIND OUT MORE

BOOKS

Hanson, Anders. *Saws*. Edina, MN: ABDO, 2010.

Nelson, Robin. *What Does a Saw Do?* Minneapolis: Lerner, 2013.

WEB SITES

eHow: How Does a Saw Work?

www.ehow.com/how -does_4690711_a-saw-work.html
Get a closer look at how different types of saws work.

How Stuff Works: Handsaws

http://home.howstuffworks.com /handsaws.htm
Look at some pictures and read more about various handsaws.

INDEX

ABOUT THE AUTHOR

Katie Marsico is the author of more than 100 children's books. She lives in a suburb of Chicago, Illinois, with her husband and children.